Here is a Block

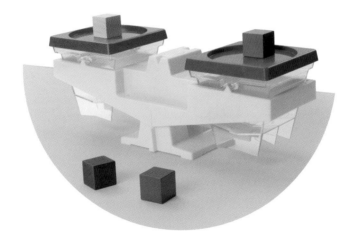

written by Anne Giulieri
photography by Ned Meldrum

Here is a blue block.
The blue block goes here.

The blue block goes down.

Here is a red block.

The red block goes here.

The red block goes down.

9

Here is a yellow block.
The yellow block goes here.

The yellow block goes down.
The blue block goes down.

Here is a green block.

The green block goes here.

The green block goes down.
The red block goes down.